Specter Mountain

MERCER UNIVERSITY

MERCER UNIVERSITY PRESS

Endowed by

TOM WATSON BROWN

and

THE WATSON-BROWN FOUNDATION, INC.

Specter Mountain

Jesse Graves and William Wright

MERCER UNIVERSITY PRESS | *Macon, Georgia*
2018

MUP/ P562

Published by Mercer University Press
1501 Mercer University Drive
Macon, Georgia 31207

9 8 7 6 5 4 3 2 1

Books published by Mercer University Press are printed on acid-free paper that meets the requirements of the American National Standard for Information Sciences—Permanence of Paper for Printed Library Materials.

ISBN 978-0-88146-653-9
Cataloging-in-Publication Data is available from the Library of Congress

This book is dedicated to Arthur Smith

Contents

Acknowledgments

Bluestem: "Gorge Storm"
Carolina Quarterly: "Cavern," "The Residual Site," "Substrata"
drafthorse: "Field-tender's Hymnal," "Ancestors"
FREE: "The Sisters"
Greensboro Review: "Confession"
Inscape: "Woodland Cathedral"
Louisiana Literature: "Overburden"
South Carolina Review: "Vessel," "Tenor at Dawn," "Salt," "Pitch," "Creek Source"
storySouth: "The First Signal," "Chthonic"
San Pedro River Review: "Blackbirds"
Still: The Journal: "Spell" (as "Mountain Spell"), "Pulse," "October Forest Inversion," "Darker Realms," "Oracle Cove"
Terrain.org: "Wild Pasture," "Epilogue [A]"
The Swamp: "The Mountain Made Anew," "Wing"

PREFACE

by ROBERT MORGAN

Co-authorship is rare in poetry, especially modern poetry. The voice of the poet is supposed to be distinct, unique. For Milton, for Blake, for the Romantics, the poet spoke as one inspired by something greater than one's self. The poet was the filament, the conductor, the medium, through which the universal energy, the vision, flowed into words and cadences. It was the individual idiom that was valued most.

In the original tradition, the oral tradition, from which our poetry comes, we know that Homer, the Beowulf poet, the Pearl poet, were writing down poems they must have heard passed on from bard to bard, each tongue embellishing, revising as it sang. So multiple authorship was very much a part of poetry from its ancient beginnings. We like to say that two heads are better than one. As folklore is the work of many through successive generations, our oldest poetry is the syncretic product of many cultures and communities.

Elizabethan playwrights often collaborated on plays, and film scripts in our time are often the work of many hands. It's well known that Joseph Conrad and Ford Madox Ford collaborated on more than one novel. There's no reason modern poets can't work together on poems. Poetry can be a craft like other crafts. Ezra Pound helped T. S. Eliot edit *The Waste Land* to become the most famous poem of the twentieth century. And Etheridge Knight and Sonia Sanchez once found synergy in writing a book of haiku together. Talents can be complementary and mutually inspiring.

Yet what Jesse Graves and William Wright have done in *Specter Mountain* is very rare. The poem begins appropriately with the language of *Genesis*, and celebrates the primal origins of the mountain, the processes of orogeny, geology. The work incorporates throughout an elemental and majestic sense of the natural, from topography to astronomy, from myth to plate tectonics. This is a poetry of air, earth, water, and fire, of storms and floods and forest fires. At times the mountain speaks for itself; at others it engages in an Emersonian dialogue, a series of questions and answers.

As we might guess from its name, Specter Mountain is haunted, both underground and above ground. It is a place of ghosts, of the dead returning in dreams, of confessions and chthonic visions. This is a world where family farms are buried under water, and worn paths slip under water and into the earth. In vivid portraits, fathers and mothers are brought back to speak to us. There are poems of confession, testimony, and witness. Some passages take the form of hymns, ballads, prayers, odes, translating the codes of nature and the mysteries of mortality. The tone is often elegiac. We pass through our days and are forgotten, though memory is haunted by the old beliefs, recalled and examined in song, in poetry. The mountain is a mausoleum, a resting place of ghosts, with sources in native American, German, and Irish culture.

But in this mountain landscape the streams are now polluted with the runoff from the meth culture. Here youths set fire to cats for fun. There seems to be a curse on the land, and hope has gone underground. The mountain refuses to prophesy. The voices of the ancestors can be heard, but they can no longer save us.

Through the many different forms of *Specter Mountain*, Graves and Wright create an oratorio effect, chorus and solo, terza rima, monologue and dialogue, hymn and elegy. There are powerful laments for brothers and fathers, ritual confrontations with the burdens of the past. The landscape may be abandoned, yet speaks with many voices.

Jesse Graves and William Wright are two of the most exciting talents in contemporary poetry. Before they have spoken in distinct and memorable individual voices. In *Specter Mountain* they have pooled their considerable gifts and found a synergy that yields a unique work that will serve as a landmark for our time, and for many years to come.

I

Prologue

[A]

And it was said unto gravity,

heave a stone
at the barren Earth that a moon will form from it—

and the worlds survived, fractured into existence.

And under the kingdoms of first waters
that kindled the leaves of the Earth, it was said:

Let the land beneath the land
move and roil, that the Earth

might lean out of dark
and light to inscribe meaning

beyond the day and night—

and so highlands and valleys churned
and streaked the land with ridge and gorge—

[B]

Old, old mountain—
elongate belts of folded and thrust
faulted
and marine, volcanic rocks
slivers of primogenital ocean floor.

One-half billion years ago, center of all
broken land masses
and in Paleozoic,
it sank and surfaced, sank and surfaced
as if in some ablution—
god of sediment and carbonate,
then
Taconic orogeny
when the mass quickened and smashed
beneath its neighbor—North American craton
            then
subduction, and Appalachia rose
enfolded in a volcanic gown
                      stippled in sandstone
and the valley's limestone
                          then
Caledonian, Acadian, Hercynian, Allegheny
orogenies, continents all thrust
and sewn as microplates swept in
                                      then
Africa crashed into North America
and pulled the mountains Himalaya-high,
                                             then
Pangea formed wholly
and drifted apart in the late Triassic—
Appalachia eroded to plain-flatness
                                                      then
resurrected in the Cenozoic unction
of streams
so fast they gnawed and slashed
through rock,
            cracked, shaped.

The First Signal

Once, down near the swales where the hay
had been doused with rain, and the bales
had come undone and lay flat and half-eaten
near the barn, my father and I walked out past

our acres into a yellow field. It was yellow
all year, a heath, and here the wood smoke came
strong. We went on walking, out past the springhouse
and the watercress on another farm, made a fire

one county over. In the paroxysms of shadow-light,
he sat there in the grass, a ghost
about to leave the body, but clung. He snapped
twigs and chucked them in the flame,

and embers blew back into his face, his hair.
He never flinched, spoke: I cannot erase my father
now for his silence, for I bear his pulse,
my own blood. I cannot transfuse love

trapped in the body and passed down, not to this land
or any creek-force or even springs when green
vines flare and speak for him, sway hymns
to vindicate the wordlessness our tongues command.

Pulse

Fathers bleed into sons, and the traveler stands
under them, under their siring shadows,
mountains casting down their glory or their gloom,
and all the finer shadings of their enfolded spirits.

Surely I have searched for striations of color
in the glistening surfaces of my father's irises,
old now and clotted as King Lear's,
pale blue, orange-flecked, opalescent.

Aeneas crossed no mountains when he
returned for his father, his frail and befallen,
his second pulse draped over his shoulders,
all former debts lofted and saved from fire,

but not forever. Even Anchises does not live
beyond his age: whatever the life on earth,
whatever the strength of the son,
who looks always in dreams, always in clouds

for the father he could not save across time.
I peer into the early-darkening sky,
listen for a voice thundering from the peaks,
watch for the signal, a falling, flaring star.

Topography

Out of the dusk that blooms
daily, out of the shadows that graft
mountain laurel and apple ridges

to the earth, sculpted by worms, owls,
campfires, and the endless snap and fall
of dying limbs; from the tortured hum

of trucks that wind their freight up
switchbacks, the shunt and steep of clouds
that fall and rise forever; out of the ores

in endless blackness that rove down
to flex in tectonic dark, the moon enters
a door that opens and closes forever. Valley floors

and karsts never dispel to dawns or noons,
and a sadness stipples earth with a clarity
only stars inhabit, that each focused eye foresees.

What is this scald of blooms, and why
the small tombs of creatures that molder
with a splendor too difficult to name?

Morning must be this bank of thorns.
Morning must be the light that dies as it is born,
a music claimed by million silences.

October Forest Inversion

Cross wet fallen chapters from the monograph
of early autumn, calibrate the spectrum of shades,
translucent yellows, burnt siennas, burnt ambers,
deep auroral reds, their simmering final language.

The footnotes of this forest tell a story,
and the story of our fathers, their bitter elements,
their soft immersions, how their work cleared
meadows and creek banks, bent their backs

into the warping shapes of aged white oak trunks.
We dig through the leaves for our own name,
burrow into the subsoil to find proof
that we lived, frail and descending as fathers.

Our mother becomes the landscape, bristle-thin
with white-wisping hair, like frostweed
spindling in the last hard breezes of autumn,
spectral in the face of winter, life's barren plain.

We follow her deeper into the wood, the chill evening,
let her guide us to where the ancestral cabins
have left no traces on the ground, where fires kept
bodies and food warm, kept life creeping forward.

Pursuit

In the swollen radiance
of this rain-soaked dawn when the sun
is no more than a rheumy eye,
sandstone and lichens begin to glow

and the mountain weeps a leaf-storm
with the day's first light, the strain every fall
fastens to the body. We've taken a wrong turn,
pulled backward into a hollow.

We careen into an echo:
Here you are, and here you will die.
Blood of the aster, blood of the boar,
the dialect of torn branch and briared hand:

blood all the same. We stagger
through vale waters, wild blazes
of bluet and jewelweed,
stumble across rivers to steeper land,

where a woman in a night gown meets us.
Her hair rolls. Her mouth is torn.
Her ears are sewn shut with thin
red yarn. She stitches

tight the hem of our conclusions.
To turn away from her is to fall
down the mountainside,
comply to gravity.

Darker Realms

My mother has taken me into the estate of her dreams,
where I may not travel alone, following steep slanting
trails from summits down into the hidden viney coves,

wet always from the mist, the dew, the seepage of roots.
She has my hand in hers, yet I feel no warmth,
no pressure of pulse beating time against pulse.

I pass through the darker solitudes of the past
like a pilgrim over foreign terrain, eyes open in the murk
but seeing nothing, then eyes closed seeing only what

her voice recalls from times before my life, recreated
through tiny forms against the back of my eyelids,
relations I have seen before in black and white pictures.

My mother leads me out of the cold, the furrowing rain,
into a room I have never beheld, unfamiliar to her, too,
except in dreams, yet she comes here often, for the dead,

to walk arm in arm again with those she loved as a child.
I will not cling to her in fear, I say with a voice not my own,
but there is no safety, and the fear brings me

to a room with a floral couch, broken down and slanting.
Two candles burn on an end-table, raising shadows
along the wet wooden floor, and there stand the figures

she brought me here to see, to clasp their hands
before they vanish into the mist, abandoning even
those stories the aged living continue to tell about them.

Confession

The pages have been ripped from the book, the spine
snapped, the cloth cover and stitching tossed in the fire.
Even if the fire consumes the roots around it,

even if this conflagration enfolds the woods
like a man doomed to kill those he loves
when he embraces them, the wind is cold, cold. My heart

is darned to a field that has lain for a long winter.
My heart has sunk with the moon into the ground,
down through granitic and basaltic layers, down

through silicates and magma that moves the lands
and waters of this Earth. But I still see the December
blue of this mountain sky, severe as a sapphire

polished and cut, lucidities that haunt the eyes
for months, belie the summer its own harassment
into deceitful fecundity, as it always does:

And since there's nothing new here, and since
the words singe and curl, give way to fragile
embers lidded by glowing seams of heat,

I will rename as winter renames; I will admit
a new narrative of ice has its say now
that all creatures are hidden in their dens:

The whip of a lizard's tail is a demon's command,
the moths' windy shaking toward any light
is mockery (their only truths unblinking when they pin

themselves to oak and elm trunks, bright as sliced agate
in the dark). Or the long unfolding of larvae
that spill from a raccoon that gnawed the toxic

gills of yellow wart and hatched for days
for its mistake. What is that save the mind
that numbs itself and even dies for a time

to stave off fear? What is that save this December
night, so cold it shakes my hands free of their blood,
free of the means to feel anything at all?

Astronomy

Let the past have its dominion tonight,
let the winded rain blow in and shake
windows loose in their softening frames,

nothing that hurt once can hurt again.
I am free to roam this land without fear,
without jealousy, intimidated by no one,

books I have studied, read again
for the first time, their words realigned
on fresh cut pages, reintroducing themselves.

Behind all those overspilling clouds, the moon
catches light still and sends it here unbidden.
I would know to ask for it if it never came,

darkness would tell me how much I need
the light, my hands outstretched.
Let the moon reap its hidden domain—

Reflected rays guide the way back, the return
to the child I once was, sitting under stars
with an uncle, a protector, guardian from fear,

who told the names of what we observed,
lifted me onto his shoulders to get us both as close
as possible to heaven, the place we believed

awaited our arrival with angels singing,
safe at last from whatever darkened visions crept
into dreams, terrors of the dead, and the living.

We traced the patterns our pointing fingers made,
star to star, map made of myths, horns, spear-tips,
flanks of a roving bear, true companions of the moon,

whose round face I loved above all other shapes
in the sky, sensing even then that her silver arrows
took aim against whatever threatened us harm.

Gatherers at Time's End, Specter Mountain

In the polar vortex, the tree limbs snapped loud
as gunshots, and I slept into a seeing of different
times, for time is an ovoid womb that gives

birth to dust, ice, and blood again and again,
that throws light back into itself until another time
is made. Numbed, I saw our towns

cities long darkened, not from cataclysm
or neglect, but from a human blossoming
toward the old utterance, the primal heart.

People scattered down the ridge
into the crimson stubble of valley to gather
around fires and sing the last words they could recall.

Snow piled on pines and blew off with rifts
of smoke. The wind still blew eastward, and the flare
of dawn still grayed into lilac into blue.

The fires forced the valley into an opening
bloom, and to hear the people singing was to know
them with love, to read them legible

as siblings. Such harmonies they made that my mouth
turned dry as years-old leaves. My body bent
into heavy narcosis. To know their rhythm

was to feel Earth gnaw at my own
measures, and to adore the world, hard as it is,
for finishing, always finishing, what it begins.

Ancient Sovereignty

The self pursues desires
that cause it grievous harm, as the redbone hound
tracks a cellular trail through briar patches,
so the ego wants what it wants, now and always,

whose sublime dream is freedom, a ship pointed
toward the horizon like a snout lifted high,
trundling the air and howling at the salt-scent.

Snow comes fluttering and the night resembles
some photograph of itself, lit from within,
shadows cast in fleeting clashing directions,
luminous as the extreme deep field of sky

hidden behind this churning wave of clouds,
behind our slow progressions of human time,
limitations of the eye, the portal telescopic.

I must find a way to sleep beneath
expanding and contracting galaxies,
to focus on the single ascending ridgeline
visible in my mind's land-sweep,

no animal life stirring as snow fills up
the bare outstretching limbs of white oak,
poplar, red maple, trembling under new weight.

I witness my footsteps there in early light,
deepest tracks on the new-fallen layer,
sinking clean through to the ice-crust
that first covered brittle leaves and twigs,

spiracle for any slight life submerged,
though only in dreams could any creature
live in the space I have imagined for it there.

Lassitude

If the body slackens, if the body rambles
sleepless through days, fatigue like dried
roses thriving from an open mouth, what can the brain

dream other than a trellis or the deep gouge
a hatchet beats into a barn wall? Once, I was
afraid of death, to become again the stuff of stars.

Now I fear my paths to the valley are blocked.
Brother, the roof crumbles over our head. Now
my ease is rocked when house plants, warm

and watered, wilt yellow and brown all
the same, their spectral breaths sealed.
Once, I was afraid of drowning. I saw myself

in dreams fall blue into a silty cradle,
down into gar and trash and the mired
leaves that flourish despite the dark.

Now I fear I shirk all the air has to give, shut myself
into the afternoons until the sun falls gold,
shuns from the heart the burdens dusk reinstates.

Vessel

Morels sprout through leaf-murk under the dead
trunk of a hickory, where almost no one can find them,
shuttered among ferns and mosses and beetle-husks,
bitter delicacy sprung from the surging current of spring.

I trouble myself to know what it is I see: I must
always look. There has never been any choice in that.
What choices have I had? I want to say none,
and the mountain will not talk me out of that.

I follow the salt-line back to origins, the trail
grown thin as a single vessel of blood,
yet I may track it up the submerged river,
through the winding gap, and back across the ocean.

History will not hold me back, but will neither reveal
all the stories my people sent to the new world,
nor whisper their voices down through the corridors
of time, though something speaks out of the darkness.

Echoes in a language I don't understand,
vibrating through the lower chambers of the heart,
how certain I have been that the trail leads me here,
back through the circle I have already followed.

Tenor at Dawn

I lend my ear to the devil tonight, to whatever voice
his dry throat musters, human or otherwise,
rasping his story of sickness across the mountain,

death keeping its white eye on those I love,
teasing them ever-closer with the whispery
fabric of his robes, the rustling silk of his veil.

All through the night clouds shift their weight,
restless to commence their falling, suspended
above the dry ground by his long curved finger,

and I watch how he withholds, how he punishes,
staying awake to hear what I imagine
he will pronounce upon the fates you pray for.

The tenor of dreams at dawn lead me
up toward the crests, ice glistening the trails
that shape your narrow passage home,

where some lifelong dread awaits my arrival,
the devil having beaten the comfort of sunrise,
his voice ringing only a cold, silent warning.

Drought's End

Summer buried spring's creatures, darkened
to the virgate core what had blossomed and writhed
in the months before. Heat-bedraggled hills

hung like stinking curtains always mildly wet, mildewed.
Farms wilted and cracked, their families gone husk and spindle,
all throats without slake. Then storms bloomed

and bombed the valleys, vanished quick as they began.
In the north pastures, lightning scorched and snatched
centuries from an oak, split now down its sole and ragged seam.

A quarter of the county came to watch the fire eat those fields
until it hit the woods, then doubled back in wind that brought
another rain to feed again the flicked latches of that tall country.

Nights brought visions of a sparrow's wickered ribs, amulets
of dragonflies near a stream that crackled over warm stone,
the softest thunder. The sun close, withered, dwindling.

Salt

Sarvis and redbud measure steep angles
with their pink and white scansion of color,
flourishing where soil clings to limestone,
where trunks curve upward like elbows,

up toward the monadnock where no trees
can hold against the wind's pressing knuckles.
The air around my body shudders with
cold breath, exhaled from opening blossoms,

root systems scrabbled over rocky ground,
salt of the ancient sea on my tongue,
and I imagine the mountain
underwater, submerged past the tree line,

fish the size of small canoes touring
through the canopy, their wide mouths
gaping high above my swiveled head.
The earth upside down, inverted time, now.

II

And It Was Said unto Water

let your rains first halo the peaks
and rejuvenate the streams that teem with fish,

but let such cycles sing through their excoriations
so that you replenish your own vessels forever

and thus the waters of the streams flowed always
through the basins to the sea,

and the clouds crept low and reverent
until their wombs broke and formed phantoms,

freed and reclaimed forever.

Chthonic

I sometimes fall into visions where the Earth
opens, and far underground, beneath the shallow dead
and the waterline, beneath any trace of life,

the world is undone, aortal and blistering,
glowing and darkening, the Hadean palpitant
center. Then, quickly, like human utterance

played backwards to clipped silence,
the world sews its wound, and all the valleys
and rivers lean again into their time-worn complexities,

flourish and die, flourish and die. Sometimes it's best
to let the dream have its say and to snuff it to silence.
Sometimes it's best to outpace the tenacious ghost

of the unconscious, lest it follow you through days.
What then is a simple solace? The stand of light
between the trees? Perhaps I love the oaks

no matter where I am—on this mountain,
behind the cabin window, or near the stream
because I cannot endure the vision

of the buried body of my grandfather—a man
I could not love for his constant mantras
about *the sinful* and *the end*. His home was nearly pitch black

even on sunny days, any light a leaking toxin.
The only comfort he found was walking fields
in the pre-dawn halflight, always looking down, down

for arrowheads and bannerstones, quartz drills,
old pipes and bottles, some evidence that he moved
and lived, that others had gone, cast off their mundane

legacies. When I was seven, he reminded me I was
going to die. His visions chased and claimed him,
buried him early. Perhaps that's why the tallness

of oaks, their susurrus glittering
through the light, yokes me with astonishment,
a love I haven't learned to name.

I did not always live so high:
Once, miles down this ridge and into the piedmont,
I had a hound that dug deep into the loam,

crazed, wide-eyed. When he had bloodied his paws
and ripped roots asunder, he found what he'd been
after: a conch shell in perfect shape, a white spiral

with pink filigree. We were hundreds of miles
from any sea. The hound now lies in a midden
in those same woods, where for years red sumac thrived

out of him, his innards and brisket,
the deepening caverns of his eyes.

Pitch

The cabin I seek leans against a tulip poplar,
half-fallen and windowless, doorless, twice as old
as the tree, last lived in almost a century ago by a man
named Richard, who married my great-aunt,

for whom the entire tract of land has been called
my whole life, and before— call it the Richard-Side—
steep and runneled with floodwater wash-outs.

Someone cared enough for the cabin at one time
to haul it six miles on the back of a wagon,
protecting it from the river-becoming-lake
that would have swallowed it like a tablet,

salvaged because someone already long dead
had been born in one of its shallow rooms,
saving the birth-spirit from a final immersion.

Does anyone remember the screams of the panther
when I was small, the human-pitched
yowling that seemed to stir up from dreams,
except that my eyes were always open

when I heard them jar the night?
Who else remembers how my brother raced home
from the woods after seeing the black streak?

Mother cat and her litter were what I imagined,
the last of something rare, alive in the hills
above my own house, so close to my window
I watched for her breath to steam the glass,

arms locked frozen around my body,
muscles tensed against the mattress, waiting,
hoping to see her shadow, and hoping not.

One morning a blue and white pick-up truck
parked along the road bank, and two men
I had never seen before carried rifles
into the woods, strangers on the Richard-Side,

and I knew what they had come for, so listened
for their shots, but all morning standing
in the yard, I heard nothing, no guns, no cries.

After that, dogs barked in the night, the familiar
voices of the half-shepherd and the hound,
but the screaming never returned, even in dreams,
even when I tried to hear it in my mind,

it was gone, when I lay with eyes pressed open,
envisioning cubs nursing her on the cabin floor,
praying to see it just once, that pitch made flesh.

Creek Source

Deer bolt from the creek, a band of six
clashing through a cluster of small cedars.
They smell their own destruction in the air,
simmering on our breaths as it reaches them.

Our ancestors and theirs flanked these banks,
watching for some trace of the other, always
hungry, reading the ground, the air, for signs.

We might have slept under their skins,
filled our mouths with their roasted shanks,
stalking them with a different intensity
than now, hoping only for a closer look.

Our fingers under-trace the water's quick-
shifting surface, close to the mineral bed,
caress past ages, unchanging.

Cold, unchanging through generations,
forests growing dense, dying,
valley of fallen oaks, blighted hemlocks,
soil enlivened by the rotting interiors.

All of it feeding the creek, surging forward
like the most alive creature in the sphere,
breathing out the coldest breath, fiercest pulse.

Ancestors

℘ Archaeology

This is what happened before the beginning,
when only the wind cut through hemlocks
and dark owls patrolled the clearings.

We know what they did for work—
digging in the ground and hacking
through trunks of trees, building rooms,

shapes in the air to hold the cold out.
They scouted and shot for food,
trading with others when they found them.

Our father cut hay in the fields closest
to the lake that now covers their first homes,
flattest bottomlands lost to flood,

while we sat at the meadow-edge
watching the tractor make its tight turns
as the ancestors must have done with mules.

We drew shapes like houses, like trees,
with a sharp stick, another in the lineage
watching the grown ones provide,

scratching the old ground with any tools
their hands could force into being,
for whatever secret life the soil offers.

℘ The Sky at Night

They brought what they knew of planting
from Rhineland mountains and dense forests,
learned how the seedtimes changed

as they followed rivers down through
Pennsylvania and across North Carolina.
What never changed was the moon,

which roots to put under ground during
the waxing phase and the waning.
Our grandfather grafted fruit trees

when we were boys. We loved
how he curled his knife into a branch,
shaving out the soft central pulp.

Cut in the dark of the moon, he said.
We loved to go out at night and look up
into the clear swirling distances,

our uncle passing a bag of candies
as we sat on the hood of his Mercury,
making up names for the constellations.

℘ Mythologies

Their cabins surrounded by woods,
they walked through forked shadows,
under the mottled light of grasping trees.

The elders scared us of any upstairs room,
water held to mirrors in candlelight,
night-time calls of strange birds.

The constricting fear they passed down
was the promise to reveal the future.
We knew of the west-flowing spring

they said foretold the death of a child,
would show the coffin we would be
buried in, signal the darkness.

The Mountain Made Anew

The mind goes its own way among the steeps,
following trails the body can never
navigate, slighter than muskrat burrows,
more hidden than the hermit thrush's nest.

Thoughts begin to sink at dusk, like shadows
hanging back, stretching away from their source,
while the fleeting sun, which abandons me
each night, ignores silent pleading for light,

for even the pink half-light that winnows
through high branches, then travels down
thickening trunks until forest density
consumes it like the flesh of fallen fruit.

The mind trades on the myth of memory,
believes it can recreate the mountain
before the fire, the trees before the blight,
valley before the flood, but solitude

cannot be trusted, the landscape evolves,
subjected like human bodies to time,
the rude wasting of old time, falling quick
upon me, or slowly, as it elects.

I carve out a remembrance, a history
that involves all I have loved, yet sense
the best lies before me somewhere,
something not yet made.

Twine

I wake early to hear your voice
spoken through the rasping wind.
I walk the valley and rejoice:
this land you always tend.

Twine me to the mountain, Lord.
Twine me to the ground.
Twine me with the grass, o Lord.
Twine me to the ground.

When I wander and hear old thunder
clap in this blowsy rain,
I know the devil tears hearts asunder—
six souls he steals and stains.

Twine me to the mountain, Lord.
Twine me to the ground.
Twine me with the grass, o Lord.
Twine me to the ground.

Till rapture comes and night grows shrill
as blood rushing through these veins,
knit my body to these hills,
steadfast to this domain.

Twine me to the mountain, Lord.
Twine me to the ground.
Twine me with the grass, o Lord.
Twine me to the ground.

Wing

I followed my own mother here—
she sang to me the whole way, just as she
always did, wherever I traveled,
with or without her, the voice that guided,

that cautioned of steep turns in the road
before I got to them, the future
foretold in the words of her plaintive hymns.

She took the huddled form of a sparrow,
shrinking within her closed wings, her chalky
sibilant calls meaning something I can
never know, nothing like her airy song,

which always says, *come, follow, come, follow,*
down from steep bluffs, toward the sloping
pastureland of my birth, true south of home.

Her body grown so thin. Her voice thinner.
A portrait hangs on a wall in the house
of memory, an upstairs room,
catching light from uncurtained windows,

her hair dark as a deep anthracite seam,
burnished black by underground pressures,
her face talc white, so young it's another life.

Her arms hover around me as a boy,
when I wore a light blue jacket, too long
in the sleeves, my curls combed straight,
gazing untroubled into the camera's eye.

Blackbirds

One late fall they descended into the valley
and amplified the bleeding trees,
cacophonies of the season's
undoing. We were afraid

that year: blackbirds often bannered
through the high air, their blurred
bodies a language kept hidden,
just beyond fluency.

Everything slackened, the kingdom
of weeds, even faith and old
tales seemed gimmickry,
the only tangibility

those blackbirds, their hive-minded
heaves from rhododendron
crowns. More than one
mind scrabbled

for some spark to snap the heart
to warmth, but nights
with the sharp stars,
those countless

distances, hazed into winter's
waking, when the morning
sun shredded to ribbons
of shadow

under the tenacious blackbirds—
and for a time the hinge
of Earth seemed locked
until those creatures

at last left us with a thin spring, long
after they'd cast dark
on our structured lores,
upset our old symmetries.

The Sisters

Brother, have you ever looked into the fire's radiance?
Have you witnessed the element up close?

What I've seen is buried deeper than the shards
that severed the floor with the flames' ranting shadows,

deeper than the first flush of the mountain's juvenescence
(for it was shallow and frost-killed), the only scents

those of ice and ash, no musky clover or apples—
deeper than summer roots or creek-wracked stones.

There in the night-delirious escape down the stairs,
hearing my old man call for us, the roof roaring to splinters—

I saw the confused yawns of my dying sisters,
the flames so loud their yells fell through the beams,

blazing; their screams turned to rattle and rictus,
teeth and the spindle-wraiths, charred to spinsters

for the mud to take and worms to harness:
Tell me, brother, have you stood high in the mountains

and watched the stars spin over meadows, dead farms
where old airs sear and douse the tongue with silence?

Fire District

People have burned this angled land for sport,
for thrill of seeing wood cinders flare,
smoke-nimbus halo above flames,

aureoles of steam and leaf spume
like bloody sickness coughed and spat,
Aurora Borealis of the simmering ridgeline.

Lightning also burns the mountainside, slashing
from Heaven, whipping scars into the backs
of Earth's colossal deformities.

Blazing in the storm, an inverted Hell
above ground, each level visible through
rising catacombs of smoke, dense mists flung

skyward against slanting cascades of rain.
Little wonder the forebears believed
dragons kept their lairs on high,

for other thoughts seemed worse,
that God would punish with living fire,
or that the devil guided the reins after all.

Offense

The crime: We bore the hound down
into the creeklands, over old pyroclastic slopes,

the dog licking your ear. Something ravaged
our boys' hearts to cruelty, our nerves violent

and church-torn. In such silences, we reasoned,
boys must silence a life at their mercy.

Then down farther into black water pooling
at lithic tuffs, then blacker water, shoulder-deep.

Mica stars wobbled deep up to our vision,
memory's celestial inversion.

We pushed down on the dog's jaw and were bitten
the muzzle snapping and forelegs flailing

in this vicious wash, a gospel we loathed
even as we sang it. The dog's teeth snarled

crazed and his throat whined a counterpoint
to birdsong and limb-chatter.

Again and again until the tongue lolled
and the crimped lips sagged, bluing.

The long-eared head sank
full and the hound's body pulled now

down a few yards to sway
where a log stayed its flow.

We carried that sin
as a bleeding hand homeward.

Steep Side Creek

Winters were colder, and come October
leaves flared, withered
quick, then bled down to dither

on the creek bottom's flow, slower, the iced-over
water sluggish, stilled. Under
the gleaming surface time sundered

late dace, crawdads, worms, salamanders
from access to the world above, flustered
as it was with mountain winds that blustered

down the watercourse, where hapless travelers
lurched with horses, the hooves' clatter
puncturing the creek's surface in spatters

of deeper water that instantly froze, a slaister
of frigid elements, small eruptions of sunlit luster
that dulled as soon as new snow fell, clustered

on the banks until Earth became harvester
of all alive, and all blood or sun-fed creatures
that could not escape froze to death, their features

paralyzed in that long cloister,
winter's endless signature,
the world's strained ligature.

Passage

For a time, the mountain emptied itself
of people, trespassers upon the land,
their herds of goats, rangy mules and cows,
chickens and bleating children, all clatter.

Choirs of redbreasts gathered to announce
province over abandoned sheds and barns,
minstrel-songs chiming through quiet cabins.

They will pick clean the unwatched orchards,
scavenging the fruit, and beetles that come
for the fruit, scouring each globe to its pit,
then nest in cold stone chimneys, new rulers

watchful from solid perches, high above
egg-puncturing teeth of the possum,
wing-shredding claws of the fleet red fox.

Some left demon-driven, spirited against,
their bibles and crosses no protection
from what seemed to accurse every turn,
human fears of the above-human world,

though money drove some away, and hunger,
and certainty that nothing could prosper
under such gales that beat upon the land.

Seeking peace, somewhere they might find it.
Specter of the steeps, permit their passage
down from your heights, past guarded vales;
pull back your shrouds of cold and mist,

so that they, never your flock, may find a trail,
depart these bare, ruined realms of dream,
to wake and find regained— attainable earth.

III

And It Was Said unto Mountains

let panicles of flowers bloom in the ravines
where the sun can speak their green languages,

and let them dry and fall in the other seasons
until ice reforms them into glittering understory

and language is engraved again by warmth
until all of its mouths spill with blooms—

thus the seasons spoke the mountain
into blossom and shadow.

Overburden

For now, the mountain is whole. For now,
the galax and foamflower bloom beyond
themselves. And when wind whorls in
the top-most branches of hickory,

a mandolin's ghosted notes
strum in a minor key. For now, the valley
meadows resume their florid sparseness,
void of any aspect of the old mountaineers

who were the last to leave, save the pine
and cedar planks of their cabins now long
collapsed, the mosses gnawing away those
sawed and hewn geometries. And in the many

doorways that open into the mountain
where the liminal craters of breath can still
be felt, just barely, one might smell pangs
of rust, salve, medicine, or soap, soon

overwhelmed by the mineral tang of stone
or petrichor. On these sheer edges
where the earth heaps or strips away,
the spring is still a seamstress, the summer

a kiln. These hills burn within
the cosmos, their deep land and the flesh it contains
filled with dimming lamps of stars. For now,
the valley's creel washes up in aster.

Wild dogs sulk under shards
of dusk the limbs reshape nightly.
Mountain lions satisfy their bloody motions.
For now, the mountain is whole.

The Residual Site

Whereupon stars cast down their blacked out husks,
so the mountain lets drop what fails to hold sap.

Trees revise their histories each year, clean growth
scripted in roots weaves a branch narrative,

new leaf, new bud, story old as ash hand-dabbed
by torchlight along a steep underground seam.

Sequoyah walked among ancestors of these woods,
his eyes following the curving symmetries

lineated in tufts of shag bark, earth verse
newly translated to a syllabary.

He made a traveling tongue, talking leaves
that could carry a message farther than the wind.

Ground water can sing its cold song forever,
but human codes go quiet after fading out,

after losing pitch to the ears of the young,
leaving a whole turn of mind, way of being,

with no voice in the world, no way to reveal
its secret truth. The mountain speaks for itself.

Questions for the Mountain

Why do you remain still in the human season?
Because your season is fleeting, and you are as broken as I.

What do you feel when your garments glow in fall?
The fire scalds me just as it would scald you.

What do you think of those who hew your sides and build?
What they build molders in one quadrillionth of a nanosecond of earth-time.

Do you not feel pain from how men have craved and carved you?
I have felt a pain beyond your reckoning.

What will I see in your creeks in the warmer seasons?
You will see what I allow you to see.

What may I witness?
Trout-curve and moss, one reading of water, one reading of stone.

What will you keep hidden?
All readings of worm, carcass, tree flux. Any true reading of water.

Why would you hide anything from me?
Because you are a mite that forms one particle of all refraction.

Why do the wild plum trees bend so low in your shadows?
Because no sun tilts there any season save the first week of spring.

How can I bear part of you away with me?
You cannot. Any stone cleaved from me is no longer my body.

Where can I hide from the fear that gnaws within me?
There are many deep swales here. There are many yawning gorges.

Have many hidden here?
Many have hidden here.

Are you then a gravestone reared up by those many sorrows?
I am a cradle, an engine, a cenotaph.

Does time move through you with greater clarity?
I suffer time a million million times over.

Are there phantoms here?
Yes, and you are one of them.

Even as I live and witness you rise with your brothers?
I speak of the man-that-is-you who moves before you move.

Are there any phantoms behind me?
More than all the stars your eyes were made to see.

Why can't I see them?
Because you are a mite that forms one particle of all refraction.

Have I hope of catching the phantom that moves before me?
Even if you do, another phantom will outpace him, then another, then another.

Forever?
Forever and ever.

Cavern

Ice finds deep pockets, sunless crevices
frozen until late spring, earliest summer.
Ground surface relents, but underground

holds clusters of crystalline slivers,
procession into further depths,
sickles hanging like porcelain fangs.

Wind practices its crude archery here.
Shafts of bitter sting fired at random,
taking down whatever finds itself

crossed between slanting currents.
Song sparrow on the ground, struck
against some unseen field of force,

quivering on the lip of the cavern,
beak working up soundless monosyllables,
wings tremble without lift, without surge.

It still moves, that stirring form which will
emerge, momentarily visible, into the light,
claim what feast air sacrifices to ground.

After Years

Nothing changes. The dead remain in their vaulted absences,
chambers built from ash and char, sod and sprouting vine.
Go ahead and speak to them, try to coax them back
into the bodied world, it will not interrupt their solitude.

Once I had an older brother who cleared the path ahead for me,
but now I must imagine that he follows an unseen track.
Go ahead and hope for that, despite no signal which would align
my wish with the expressionless sky, or its unspooling silences.

My brother has been to the room our mother visits,
where those figures lost in time await some unrevealed sign
to ascend from their lower realms, past hovering black
waves of clouds, out of the murk and into the blue.

Nothing changes, and no matter how many years pass,
the room sinks further beneath an ashen watermark.
No ferryman waits to deliver us into some benign
realm of the dead, past home and future presences.

Gorge Storm

Better to keep faith
in the mystery
of all this black ridge, rising to fog.

Better to walk the mind through the deep
gorge, cluttered with bitter apples,
the summer-rotten branches choked
pungent by the damp cold.

ᘓ

Dear God,
let me get up. Let me crest this rain.

Let this wind become a kingdom;
the bindweed a prayer:

> *Let the sternum grow slack,*
> *the face stiffen,*
>
> *the ligaments, tissues, and all*
> *organs break*
>
> *to stone. And let the stone*
> *of the new body crack*
>
> *open to the diamonds of our blooms,*
> *our silver veins pulsing.*

ᘓ

Two centuries ago, the horses fled.
The shed collapsed, and the farmhouse's walls
grew ripe with mold. One stand of corn still grew, warped,
in the north pasture.

Crows snipped the ears bear.
Possums skulked
to lower land. The family lay
ever in their beds.

Alliance

Life on the mountain was a tale of belief and doubt,
punishment for sins borne out or envisioned in dreams,
levied down by some ruler beyond the ragged peaks,
beyond the briefly visible ball of the sun.

Give friction its story to tell, setting wind against slate,
water against limestone, bird against bush,
where natural allies oppose one another to the end.

Life on the sea is twisted no less contrary to itself,
waves shredding loose boards, shaving away all excess
into a fine mist of particle, a slight spray of foam,
like fog billeted in bare branches of winter trees.

Brother, have you been to the shore and watched fleet ships
assemble into splaying armadas, form quadrants
so numerous your eye will not receive them all?

Only in books. Only in the world of heavy antiquity
can you find such a scene fixed in amber,
fixed tight in the globe of the mind's detached eye,
morning's golden steed harnessed by the gods.

Seduced by some token worn between the breasts
even sleep and night cannot resist, we must allow
resistance to tell the story of its own conception.

Once void adjudicated. No other emerged for eons.
Then a swirl of sexual doom, variation:
from love is born light, from night is born nemesis,
neither at liberty to proceed without the other.

The world is a deep well, and to lay at the edge
peering down into its vaster chasms is to live
under the mausoleum of the mountain.

Woodland Cathedral

Something very old speaks outward
from October's first cold nights,
voice original to burning wood,
ember-seethe, smoke-whisper,

stars behind veils of nightcloud
shimmer unseen, shimmer
unseen above watchful trees,

ghost-wolves outside the circle
of firelight, witness to the burning,
last vestige of rituals carried
across an ocean and over mountains,

meadow as throne room,
voice descendent of ancient offerings
proffered to soil, seedling, sky.

Revenants

Some children endured terrible fates,
chased by two panthers, one black
and one gold, who leapt into air

above the child's head, climbing
one another up into the sky,
fur flying until nothing was left.

Snakes twined around the ankles
of boys and girls walking to the garden,
sent after tomatoes and squash,

green snakes that tied the children
together and dragged them up a tree.
They could fall into practically anything,

pits appearing where there had been
solid ground, shafts of light cast down
into the dark, into deep watery troughs

where ancient fish hovered eyeless.
Water whispered terrible secrets
about when they would die, and which

forests their ghosts would roam through,
always seeking the hidden answer
to how they could live in the afterlife,

make death their servant,
life their vanishing burden.
Death the eternal servant.

Substrata

So much time for dark envisionings,
rock crystals forming in the mind,
solidifying into permanent structures.

To survive February is an accomplishment
in this family, the future hiding behind
banks of fog, only the unknown ahead,

green bottom-fields covered with water,
ice along the edges, where the past looks
like a pasture with fat grazing cattle.

Eastern hardwood forests cast shadows
over whole lifetimes, even if they are short,
even if we are outlived by the overhanging trees,

their shadows following us underground,
deep into the substrata, the water table
rising around our bones, all our sodden parts.

Field-tender's Hymnal

My pair of draft-horses scuff the rails
of their stables, the children have eaten
stewed potatoes and bread, and play now
under the Dutch elms' reaching shade.
They chase chickens and geese,
and it pleases me to watch them
make such trouble while I drink
from a warm cup on the front bench.
This ground we tend will belong to them,
so I teach what they are ready to learn,
how to furrow the fields without run-off,
to watch the moon for signs to plant.
Soon I will call them in, light the candles.
We will read from St. Matthew's Passion,
first me, then their mother, then each child
until time for sleep, when I will take a final turn
at reading while their eyes settle into rest.
The candles we do not make at home,
for those we must trade in the far village,
like the Heidelberg of our former lives.
We will not burn the wicks long for pleasure,
just a few more verses, until the music
I hear after saying these words aloud
rises to the chorus, voices that carry me
into dreams of high-stacked hay,
each grown boy driving his own team,
the light of long suffering warming it all.

Old Woman

She scythed the field where land grew wild,
steep pasture edge that held the bones
of horses, now stoked, recompiled

to tufts of white blooms, pauson sewn
on this pasture ridge. She sliced low
and long until dusk loomed, postponed

her toil, then leaned home, the flow
of sun now sealed by moth and star,
sky bathed in dark, adagio

and nocturne of sheer calm, a name
the night owned whole, that coldest song.
She propped the scythe against the frame

of the barn, where she smelled the pong
of fraught days hard lost—sap, dung, nail—
and most pungent the cedar's long

bruised scent. Her world all rasp and wail,
board by board, seed by seed, calloused
life nearly choked by scarce rain, failed

summer crops, her faith a cracked chalice.
So many years her bones ached such
that she felt her body split, palace

crumbling, cuts, welts she winced to touch
with salve. The yields enough to keep
her starved, she lived on, and clutched

sparse memory, no vim to weep
over spouse or child she long outlived,
the last the mountain let her reap.

Spell

It comes to me in fragments, a magnificent dark
and a final sense I belong

to wild onion and sassafras and other divinations
of autumn stems—

Each day I'll fall to it, chewing my lips
till they bleed, and my right hand

trembles cold as though it is submerged
in the old wild Shannon

of my long-dead kin, and I will see
the sky wilt like a lilac flower

and a thunder will come, more a bell
than a rumble—and I have told

only you, for I find it no devilment—
I need no demon-siphoner,

for this magic comes from some history
twisting up bright and green

and I wish for it to keep on placing
on my tongue the charged sweetness

of honey, and I wish for it to shake me
till my eyes rattle in my head like a gourd—

and I wish for it to raise my sleep
into the glory of a deep rain

all night, until I wake and bear again
morning's broken clarity.

Oracle Cove

This briar trail has delivered you,
traveler, into the hidden plexus
of the forest, artesian wellspring

speaking in swift rippling elision,
natural language long forgotten
in the tongue's narrow channels.

You believe deeper galaxies exist
than this one, spinning frenetic,
rotating through grooved orbits,

auroras, cascades, effusions,
oceanic movements in tiny
drops of mist, drops of light.

The sound compares to nothing,
not birds singing, not rain
rivering off slanted ridgetops.

This mountain refuses to know you,
to tell the future you hope awaits,
which is plain: the child in time

moves in each direction, greeted
by mothers and fathers of past life,
foreseeing all those you will become.

What is the origin of this water
that trickles from the mouth
of a forever buried cove, and fills

all the floors of the ancient seas?
How will you translate the voice
that beckoned you to this dark pit,

this oracle, its message unrevealed?
Light from the moon cannot penetrate
the canopy overhead, frost at midnight

unseen, but felt along deep tissue,
not knowing whether you climbed
upward or descended to arrive here,

knowing neither the origin nor
the destination, compelled by force
into the immense heart of the mountain.

IV

Epilogue

The water's gone
that married time and loved the stone
into a canyon's grace. We've forgotten
how to stay—how to say: *this place.*
—Betty Adcock

The apples falling like great drops of dew
to bruise themselves an exit from themselves.

And it is time to go, to bid farewell
to one's own self, and find an exit...
—D. H. Lawrence

Mother

Mother of this valley, the moss and fern
wilt in drought; the sun wrests water
to trickling shadow.

The mountain kneels. The seep creaks
stone with benzodiazepine,
a stranded trout with phosphine

sediment. Down a mile, the silt
slags with runoff from a meth house
where water falls harder

from an incoming rivulet
to create broken confluence,
suds that shake dark with erosion.

Mother of this valley, the wind
mists the air creatureless,
the wind winds a chain

around the throat
of a saw-whet owl. After rain,
the stone reeks: nail polish

and the insoluble
unction of rust.

All Kin

Finally, the cabin falls
where a man might have lived alone
for near a century, his nights

led by candlelight and hunger—
finally, he enters the third death:
all memory winters him

into the eventual
blindness of all past.
In autumn, sparrows land

on this rubble, their winter
colors grafted onto rafters,
warped wood rot and sparrow plank

folded into the mud and mold
of dimmed memory,
precise tones of the passing self.

The Estranged

Somewhere in the flatlands
a woman rots in a shallow grave,
dumped sometime last summer

by the truck-bed boys of a silent town,
where violence buds in their hearts
like pulsing nettles, brown calculi

of hard drugs knitted between
their teeth. They smile with a blade's exactness.
Nights they piss in the gardens

of strangers and light cats on fire,
laugh at the pain and yowls and shudder,
and the slow boy who scorches

a British shorthair's tail and gets the blue of his iris
gouged and raked red by the terrified claw
is slapped by the others, just because

pain and fear is the engine that ignites
their cruelties. They lurch
through woods,

come to the trailers and shatter
glass bottles against their own walls
until they settle back into their traps,

paths that circle
round and round the same place,
that cuff their scarred hands to home.

This is not a fiction; this is hidden
fact, the petrified senses of those
who look away for good.

You might say: *But beauty still*
scuttles through these impediments.
You might say: *Why fixate*

on their enfeeblement when time itself
is the grand erosion? The mountain
will answer quick.

Father

Dear father-of-this-mountain, my father,
I have no story to tell. I have few words
to say while the ants infest and bear
away the lynx's carcass and maggots

sprout to eat away every last morsel of self.
When my ear hits the pillow, I hear only
my pulse—it betrays everything, offers
no wise gossip. It thrives alone.

Nights I dream you under an overcast sky,
somewhere on the southeast slope,
tucked in a pocket of hemlock
where the streams converge

into quick rushes before long winter rains
slow downstream, the water clear,
bearing up to sight every stone.
Father, I dream of underwater

rivers, my vision wavering, the moon
big as a chine. I dream within this dream,
become a rainbow trout dashing
into water grasses, then a bear prowling

through diamond hedges of new snow.
And when I become the creature
with eyes that can decode your form,
you shatter and fall like winter into all valley meadows.

Father-of-nothing, I am the product
of Bible and babble, of glossolalia
thrown against moon and mountain—
both throwing any utterance back,

for they are too are echoes. Father,
there's thunder coming over the lower pasture—
there's fire coming over the ridge,
hymns of ablution, of effacement.

Father, I love you. You are not a wilderness.
You are not the fox that lopes away. The valley is not
a cradle. The valley is silence so complete
it blares through the hills a woeful howl.

Brother

Brother, who knits the winters
with dour albs of rain?

Who taps the stamen and milksap,
untethers the sleeping seed?

Brother of barns and lordly muscles
of horse pasture, it is time

to say goodbye—the white trees
rise to bluest morning, the austral slowness

of spring. This is a darkening,
too: the silver peach blossoms

laden by gravity and pesticides,
histories, stone and rust, bone and blood

and well before when these hills formed and stretched
higher than the Alps. The millennia rolled on

and shaped the rock that we now reshape.
We choke all-time

for our single hour. The land
has not yet said all it must say—

one syllable of its utterance
is slower than one thousand summers.

Brother, we get older; time quickens,
disperses, starlings at the field's edge.

Memory becomes seasonless,
strange, and the bloodroot

curdles to foam near the river.
Brother, before we part,

let's walk one last time
down to watch the creek,

where vestige apples
melt to sugared slurry,

stunted by the mass
of their own beginning.